CANAL RECOLLEC

CANAL
RECOLLECTIONS

JULIAN HOLLAND

PARKGATE
BOOKS

CANAL RECOLLECTIONS

Front cover photograph: *A scene full of period detail at Brentford, Grand Union Canal, circa 1930.*

Back cover photograph: *Mersey Weaver Company's boats* Aboukir *(No. 156),* Punch *(No. 159) and* Holland *(No. 100), wait at the top of the Anderton Lift, Trent & Mersey Canal, circa 1930.*

Half title page photograph: *Christening scene aboard the butty* Elaine *at Buckby on the Grand Junction Canal in 1910. The butty was owned by Messrs. L. B. Faulkener, long-distance canal carriers who were based at the Leighton Buzzard yard which is now occupied by the Wyvern Shipping Company. Buckby, a short distance from Norton Junction where the Leicester section of the Grand Union Canal branches off the Main Line, was once famous for the boatman's shop which sold beautifully decorated, traditional water cans. Today, the New Inn is still a popular canalside pub at Buckby Top Lock.*

Title page photograph: *Regent's Canal Dock with BWB narrow boats* Padbury *and* Downham, *motorised boats* Baldock *and* Rufford *being loaded directly from the motor vessel* Milborne, *circa 1960. Sadly, this busy scene has long since disappeared and Limehouse Basin, as the dock is known, has been redeveloped with a marina.*

First published in Great Britain in 1998
by Parkgate Books Ltd,
Kiln House,
210 New Kings Road,
London SW6 4NZ
An imprint of Collins & Brown Ltd
Text © Parkgate Books Ltd
All photographs © British Waterways

British Library Cataloguing in Publication Data:
A CIP catalogue record for this book is available from the
British Library.

ISBN 1-85585-396-5

Photo research and text by Julian Holland
Creative director: Julian Holland
Designed by Nigel White
Colour reproduction by Global Colour Separation Ltd.
Printed and bound in China by Sun Fung Offset Binding Company Limited.
Produced in association with Hanway Press, London.

INTRODUCTION

Imagine what the canal builders of the 18th and 19th centuries would think of the uses that the fruits of their labours would be put to, two hundred years later? How strange and rather wonderful that their legacy is now used by thousands of people enjoying their leisure time and that the ribbons of water that once served the dark satanic mills would become linear wildlife habitats. And who knows, when the motorways are totally gridlocked and oil runs out, what the environmentally friendly and pollution-free canals will be used for? Is it too much to hope that the works of Brindley, Telford and Jessop could become the silent and clean motorways of the future?

The history of Britain's inland waterways goes back to the Roman occupation when engineers built the Fossdyke to link the Rivers Witham and Trent. By the beginning of the 17th century there were several

Thomas Clayton was one of the last operators of commercial canal boats on the Birmingham Canal Network. Their base was at Oldbury on the short Titford Canal, reached via a flight of six locks, known as 'The Crow', from the Old Main Line of the BCN. In this 1950s photograph Clayton's boats Gifford *and* Severn *lie alongside each other opposite one of the company's rotting hulks at Oldbury. Clayton's boats carried cargoes of liquid tar and gas water to the local tar distillery until the mid 1960s. The Titford Canal was built in 1837 and was once very busy serving many local wharves and industries. It now ends at Titford Pools, an area of water overlooked by the tall stilts of the M5 motorway.*

hundred miles of navigable rivers in England, including the River Lee and the River Welland. 150 years later this mileage had risen to well over a thousand and included the Upper Thames, River Wey, River Severn and Hampshire Avon. Of these the Severn was by far the most important and was one of the busiest waterways in Europe.

With the advent of the Industrial Revolution the need to transport large quantities of raw materials, especially coal, to the industrial centres of the Midlands and North of England soon concentrated the minds of industrialists and engineers. The existing road system was antiquated and the steam engine and railways were still a century away. The Canal Age in Britain was born of this acute need for reliable long distance transport. The success of several schemes on the Continent in the late 17th century pointed the way forward. The first major canal in the British Isles was the 18-mile Newry Canal, opened in 1741 to link the coalfield of Coalisland in County Tyrone to Newry.

The first canal to be built in England was the 8-mile St Helens Canal, opened in 1757 with 10 locks. This was soon followed in 1761 by the opening of the Bridgewater Canal, generally acknowledged as being the first of the 'modern' canals in England. The Bridgewater was initially built to carry coal from the Duke of Bridgewater's coal mines at Worsley to the growing industrial city of Manchester. The canal, engineered by James Brindley, was both an engineering and financial success. Brindley was the first of several renowned canal engineers and following on the heels of his success with the Bridgewater Canal he was soon employed on the construction of the Trent & Mersey as part of a network of canals designed to link the major cities and industrial centres of England. The construction of the Trent & Mersey included the building of the notorious Harecastle Tunnel. When completed in 1777, five years after Brindley's death, the 1¾-mile tunnel was one of the greatest engineering achievements of the time.

By the end of the 18th century, Canal Mania had gripped the country. Great canal engineers, including Thomas Telford, John Rennie, and William Jessop were soon employed in the construction of hundreds of miles of waterways. At the time some of the major engineering features pushed known technology to its limit. What is amazing is that these canals were all built without machines. Up to 50,000 'navigators' or navvies roamed the country, causing mayhem in their wake for the local population.

A tranquil scene in Blisworth Cutting, Grand Junction Canal, circa 1920. Two horse-drawn loaded butties approach the northern end of Blisworth Tunnel.

Workmen pose for the camera while repairing fittings to a lower lockgate on the Grand Junction Canal, circa 1905. In the early 19th century these locks were excavated manually by teams of navvies. Locks transport boats from a lower water level to a higher level or vice versa. A pair of massive lock gates, usually made of oak and opened manually by massive oak paddles, are located at either end of the brick-lined chamber.

By the early 19th century a network of canals linked all of the important industrial and population centres of England. In the Birmingham area alone, over 100 miles of canals had been built to serve the fast-growing industries of the Black Country. Due to the difficult terrain, fewer canals were built in Wales and Scotland. However, reference must be made to one of the engineering feats of this period - the Caledonian Canal. The canal is in reality a series of natural lochs linked together by man-made cuts. It was designed by William Jessop and constructed jointly by him and Thomas Telford. Its opening in 1822 meant that ships could travel across Scotland from east to west, and vice versa, without having to make the hazardous sea voyage around Cape Wrath.

Sadly, two factors were to cause the canals' early downfall and decline soon set in.

Firstly, there had been no standardisation in the width of the canals. Some, such as Brindley's Staffordshire & Worcestershire Canal were built as narrow canals, with locks only 7ft 6in wide. Brindley insisted on narrow canals for economy of construction and alleviation of water supply problems. Others, such as the Leeds & Liverpool, were built to accommodate wide beam boats. Where goods had to be transported across several canal systems their trans-shipment from one boat to another obviously caused great delay and inconvenience.

Secondly, the advent of railways, with their speedier service and, apart from the Great Western Railway until 1892, their standardisation of gauge, was the final death knell for the canals. The canal companies fought back with lower tolls and modernisation schemes but it was all too late. The one exception was the opening of the Manchester Ship Canal in 1894. Using state-of-the-art steam-powered mechanical diggers this vast engineering project enabled sea-going ships with a deadweight of up to 12,500 tons to reach the centre of Manchester.

In the meantime, many of the struggling canal companies were taken over by the competing railways who, understandably, did nothing to improve matters. By the beginning of the 20th century the decline was irreversible and many canals were closed or had become unnavigable. Even an

The fore'ard end of the interior of former passenger packet boat Duchess Countess *as she was in 1950. This cramped but comfortable space gives some idea of living conditions aboard a typical working narrow boat. To the left is the coal-fired range which could provide hot water, heating and cooking for an entire family. An excellent 1/16 scale model of this boat, in its original form, can be seen in Manchester Museum.*

amalgamation in 1929 of several independent canal companies, of which the Grand Junction was the largest, to form the 300-mile Grand Union Canal failed to halt the decline. Nationalisation of half the system followed in 1948 and by the 1960s commercial traffic had virtually ceased to exist. Today, the only meaningful commercial traffic can be seen on the Aire & Calder Canal where 'Tom Puddings', or trains of barges, still convey bulk loads of coal and oil to power stations.

However, since the 1960s there has been a canal renaissance with the growing use of the remaining system for leisure purposes. To cope with this increasing demand major restoration schemes have reopened many disused canals in recent years. The disused southern section of the Stratford-upon-Avon Canal, taken over by the National Trust in 1960, was the first canal in Britain to be restored by a volunteer labour force when it reopened in 1964. A picturesque stretch of the Monmouthsire & Brecon Canal followed in 1970 and the Kennet & Avon Canal was completely reopened between Reading and Bristol in 1990. Many restoration schemes are either in hand or planned and include the following canals: Basingstoke, Dudley No. 1, Chesterfield, Dearne & Dove, Edinburgh & Glasgow Union, Forth & Clyde, Grantham, Huddersfield Narrow, Montgomery, Neath, Rochdale, Stroudwater/Thames & Severn, Swansea, Wey & Arun and Wilts & Berks.

The Canal Age has also left a wonderful legacy of architectural and engineering gems that will be marvelled at by generations to come. Of these, probably the most amazing wonders of the canal world are the Bingley Five Rise staircase locks on the Leeds & Liverpool Canal, Pontcysyllte Aqueduct on the Llangollen Canal, the Anderton Vertical Lift on the Trent & Mersey Canal and the 3¼-mile Standedge Tunnel on the Huddersfield Narrow Canal.

The future for canals now looks rosier. With the growing awareness of wildlife conservation, Britain's canals provide a wonderful linear wildlife habitat. In city centres, such as Birmingham, previously disused canals and canalside buildings have been beautifully restored, breathing life back into these previously dank and dismal surroundings. Restored canal towpaths are now used extensively for walking and fishing. Marinas have sprung up all over the system providing amenities for the ever-increasing number of leisure boats. Perhaps, one day in the not too distant future, the ghosts of Brindley, Telford and Jessop will witness the story of Britain's canals turning full circle when commercial goods are once again carried from London to Birmingham or Liverpool to Leeds.

In this book, with the aid of the extensive archive collection of British Waterways, we have tried to portray life on Britain's canals from the late 19th century to the 1960s. What stands out is the sheer dedicated hardwork, often in miserable, damp and dangerous conditions, of the British boatpeople. In particular, a boatwoman's life was hard and included raising a family, keeping the boat spick and span, cooking meals, steering the boat, loading and unloading the boat, knitting and washing clothes. All in a day's work!

Julian Holland
Glastonbury, 1997

COSTUMES OF THE BOAT PEOPLE

A pair of Fellows, Morton & Clayton butties with horse, boatmen and women in traditional costume, Grand Junction Canal, circa 1900. At the end of the 19th century the hardworking boatwomen wore a very distinctive costume that consisted of an ankle-length skirt covered by a long apron and an ornate blouse surmounted by a shawl. Their equally distinctive headgear was a stiff bonnet, usually black, topped with elegant tucks and gathers. At the back was a long curtain to protect the neck from the sun.

Above: *Fellows, Morton & Clayton steam-powered narrow boat No. 54, Phoenix, on the Grand Junction Canal, circa 1900. This photograph clearly illustrates the ornate decorations that adorned these working craft and the distinctive clothes of the hardworking boat people.*

Left: *A canal boat lass. This studio photograph, taken in 1910, clearly shows the traditional dress of a boatwoman on the Grand Junction Canal. She is carrying one of the highly decorated Buckby water cans and a cracking whip which was used to keep the towing horse on the move. A boatwoman's life was hard and included raising a family, keeping the boat spick and span, cooking meals, steering the boat, loading and unloading the boat, knitting and washing clothes. No wonder that they needed to be strong lasses!*

BASINGSTOKE CANAL

Above: *Renewing the lower gates and digging out silt at Brookwood Lock, Basingstoke Canal, circa 1912. Opened in the 18th century to link the market town of Basingstoke with the River Thames via the Wey Navigation, the Basingstoke Canal was in a poor state of repair for much of this century. Until the 1950s it was navigable as far as the collapsed Greywell Tunnel and commercial traffic continued to Woking until 1949. After this date the canal became silted up and the locks needed repair. More recently the Surrey and Hampshire County Councils compulsorily purchased the canal and it is now restored as far as Greywell Tunnel, near North Warnborough.*

Left: *The last desperate attempt to get through to Basingstoke on the weed-choked Basingstoke Canal in 1913. The boat, appropriately named* Basingstoke, *was owned by A. J. Harmsworth & Sons of Aldershot.*

REGENT'S CANAL

Above: *A busy 1930s scene of Regent's Canal Dock with numerous lighters loaded with coal. Limehouse Basin, as the dock is now known, was opened in 1820 when the Regent's Canal was completed. This 8½-mile canal links the River Thames at Limehouse to the Paddington Arm of the Grand Union at Little Venice. The canal, once busy with extensive commercial traffic, winds its secretive way through a landscape of old wharves and warehouses. Regent's Canal Dock covers an area of 11 acres and was once the London terminus of the Grand Union Canal Company. Sea-going ships of up to 3,000 tons could enter the dock from the River Thames through the Limehouse Ship Lock. Their cargoes of coal, timber and building materials were offloaded into the canal boats and barges for transport, via the Regent's and Grand Union Canals, to destinations as far north as Manchester. The Dock was closed to shipping in 1970 and has since been developed as a marina.*

Right: *Smoke drifts across Regent's Canal Docks as Associated Canal Carriers' narrow boats await transhipment of goods from sea-going vessels, circa 1932. Among the waiting boats are* Josephine, Alexandra, Edward, Anne, Henry, Swallow *and* Baron.

Above: *A very posed photograph of a lock keeper with lady and small boy at Camden Locks, Regent's Canal, 1948. Note the serge coat with Grand Union Canal Company's initials on the lapel. Camden Lock today is a fascinating canal centre set amidst the hustle and bustle of north London. Boat trips operate from here to Little Venice and the former warehouses now accommodate television and radio studios and a popular weekend market.*

Left: *A busy scene at Regent's Canal Dock, circa 1930. In the foreground are boat* Henry *and butty No. 12311* Anne *in Associated Canal Carriers livery, whilst behind them are boats* Edward *and* Alexandra *in Grand Union Canal Carrying Company livery.*

A 7hp petrol driven tractor hauls a timber-laden dumb lighter between Islington and Hampstead Road, Regent's Canal, 1953. These tractors, introduced in 1925, were a more efficient alternative to traditional four-legged power as they were able to haul two barges instead of one, with a fifty per cent saving in time. However, horses still continued to be used until the 1950s.

LIVING ON A NARROWBOAT

Mrs Lapworth and her young child on the British Waterways butty Cheam *at Brentford in 1955. Butty boats were unpowered and were either horse-drawn or, in later years, towed behind a motorised boat. They were steered by a large wooden rudder fitted to a curved tiller. The cramped cabin accommodation, no more than 12ft in length, often had to provide living space for a whole family. Cooking and hot water was provided by a small coal-fired range fitted with a hinged chimney that was lowered to allow passage of the boat below low bridges. Forward of the cabin was the main hold, often sheeted with tarpaulins, and beyond that a small foredeck which provided storage space for ropes, horse feed and tackle. These boats remained virtually unchanged for 150 years and were not phased out of service until the early 1960s.*

GRAND UNION CANAL - LONDON

Above: *Sabey's boats* Abbeville *and* Southwold *at the loading wharf adjacent to Willesden Power Station in the 1930s. The site is located on the Paddington Arm of the Grand Union Canal. The Arm was opened to traffic in 1801 and links the Regent's Canal at Little Venice with the Grand Union Canal at Bulls Bridge Junction, a distance of nearly 14 miles. Today, the Arm is a peaceful ribbon of water cutting through the industrial suburbs of north west London. The Grand Junction Arms public house in Willesden is a popular canalside pub.*

Right: *A scene full of period detail at Brentford, Grand Union Canal, circa 1930. In the foreground is Toovey's decorated wide boat* Golden Spray *built by Bushell Bros. of Tring. Brentford is at the southern end of the Grand Union Canal and is linked with the tidal River Thames by Thames Locks. Originally opened as the Grand Junction Canal, the section from Brentford to Braunston (apart from the troublesome Blisworth Tunnel) was opened in 1800.*
Until the 1960s, Brentford, with it's large warehouses, was a busy interchange point between the River Thames, railways and the canal. Today, Brentford Dock Marina caters for the ever increasing numbers of canal pleasure boats. To the west of the canal at this location is the 16th century Syon House and the grounds of Syon Park, laid out by Capability Brown in the 18th century.

GRAND UNION CANAL CARRYING COMPANY

'Royalty' class narrow boats being completed for the Grand Union Canal Carrying Company at Woolwich in the 1930s. Until 1934 the G.U.C.C.Co. was known as Associated Canal Carriers, originally a small company based in Northampton that was taken over by the Grand Union Canal Company in 1930. During the 1930s the company embarked on a massive boat building programme, increasing its fleet from 14 pairs of boats to 200 pairs. However, due to the increasing competition from rail and road transport this modernisation was too late and traffic on the canals continued to decline.

Grand Union Canal Company's three-wheeler service vehicle attending to G.U.C.C.Co. boat Merope in 1935. Until nationalisation in 1948 the Grand Union Canal Carrying Company was a major traffic concern, serving many towns in the Midlands directly by water or by a fleet of lorries connecting with the boats. By the late 1930s the company had developed the largest fleet of narrow boats in Britain. The narrow boat in this photograph carried the number 64 and was registered at Rickmansworth.

BOAT CHILDREN

Above: *The Boatmen's Institute at Brentford in 1905. This building was erected by the former Grand Junction Canal Company as a mission to local boat people. It housed a school for boat children who can be seen in their classroom in this photograph taken in 1912 (right). Here, boat children were educated while their parents' boat was laid up for loading or unloading. The Institute can still be seen a short distance from the canal in a 19th-century square called The Butts.*

Above: *Boat children at Stoke Bruerne in the 1930s.*

Left: *At Bull's Bridge Junction, the intersection of the Grand Union Canal main line and the Paddington Arm, education was provided in a converted barge. In this photograph, circa 1930, boat children and their teacher can be seen hard at work in the Elsdale barge school.*

Right: *An idyllic scene of boat children relaxing under the trees on the side of Blisworth Cutting, Grand Junction Canal, circa 1925. Due to the haphazard education provided for these children many of them remained illiterate. A child's life afloat could also be arduous, sometimes dangerous and they were often called upon at an early age to assist with work on the boat. A child from a large family might even be hired out to another boat family who were short of crew.*

A boat child of the 1950s.

GRAND UNION CANAL

Above: A 1930s scene at Grove Church Lock on the Grand Union Canal, 1½-miles south of Leighton Buzzard. Ted Barrett Jnr. is the steerer of Samual Barlow's ornately decorated butty John *as it navigates through the lock. Attractively grouped around the lock, set in the beautiful valley of the River Ouzel, are a lock keeper's cottage, bridge and a small 14th century church.*

Left: An animated scene at Norton Junction in the 1930s where the Grand Union Canal Carrying Company's narrow boats Fornax *and* Ra *are being 'gauged' for tolls. Norton Junction is where the Leicester section of the Grand Union Canal branches away from the main line from London to Birmingham. Immediately to the east lies the corridor formed by Watling Street, the M1 motorway and the Euston-Glasgow main railway line. A short distance to the south east of the junction lies Buckby Top Lock and the popular New Inn canalside pub. Sadly, the nearby boatman's shop, once famous for its hand-painted water cans, is now closed.*

MAINTENANCE WORK

Above: *Road surfacing with a steam roller on newly strengthened bridge No. 2 on the Northampton Arm of the Grand Junction Canal, 1912. The picturesque 5-mile long Northampton Arm opened in 1815 and provides a link between the present Grand Union Canal at Gayton Junction with the River Nene at Northampton. A major feature of the canal is the flight of 13 locks at Rothersthorpe which today are overshadowed by the busy M1 motorway bridge to the north.*

Left: *Traditional methods of lockwork in progress at Osterley Lock on the Grand Junction Canal, circa 1910. The scene today at Osterley is dwarfed by the large embankment of the M4 motorway. The River Brent joins the canal at nearby Hanwell Locks and follows the same course to the Thames at Brentford. Several weirs along this stretch, including one at Osterley, are a noted hazard for canal boats. Immediately to the west of the lock is the beautiful parkland of Osterley House, built in the 16th century and internally decorated by Robert Adam in the 1770s.*

FOXTON INCLINE

Above: *Local dignitaries inspecting the operation of a steel caisson on the occasion of the opening of the Foxton Incline. The Foxton staircase locks on the Leicester Section of the Grand Union Canal opened in 1812 and raised the canal over 70ft. They were temporarily bypassed by this inclined plane which opened in 1900. The plane worked on a system of counter-balanced steel caissons which were hauled up the incline on rails by a steam winch, but due to high running costs and unreliability it was closed in 1911 to be replaced by the original locks. The inclined plane, eventually broken up in the late 1920s, is now the subject of complete restoration by the Foxton Inclined Plane Trust. Formed in 1980 the Trust's long term aim is the complete restoration of the inclined plane, which has been derelict for most of this century.*

Right: *The butty* Blisworth *being lowered on the Foxton Incline, circa 1900.*

The short-lived, newly completed Foxton Incline in 1901 with the two loaded caissons passing midway on the hill.

DREDGING

A Grand Union Canal Company's hand-dredging boat in the 1930s. Dredging canals was a continuous task that was necessary to stop the waterways silting up and becoming impassible. The early dredging boats were spoon dredgers that were worked solely by manpower. On these boats a gang of three men were capable of clearing about 30 tons of silt in a day. At the end of the 19th century, steam power was introduced to operate spoon dredgers, grab dredgers and continuous chains of buckets.

COSGROVE AND THE BUCKINGHAM ARM

Lockwork in progress using sheerlegs and horses at Cosgrove Locks on the Grand Junction Canal in 1900. Half a mile to the south is the cast-iron Great Ouse Aqueduct which carries the canal over the River Ouse. The aqueduct was built in 1811, replacing an earlier structure designed by William Jessop that collapsed in 1808. Cosgrove was formerly the junction with the long abandoned Buckingham Arm. This 10-mile long branch last saw commercial traffic in the late 1930s. The picturesque village of Cosgrove contains canal warehouses, an unusual Gothic-style bridge built in 1800 and the popular Barley Mow canalside pub.

*Loading harvest direct to boat on the
Buckingham Arm in the Maids Morton area,
circa 1900. These boats were often fitted with
additional side planks thus enabling a wider load
to be carried. Opened in 1801, the Buckingham
Arm was a 10-mile long branch from Cosgrove
on the Grand Junction Canal. It last saw
commercial traffic in 1938 and was officially
abandoned in 1961. More recently a short section
from Cosgrove to Old Stratford has since
been restored.*

STOKE BRUERNE AND BLISWORTH TUNNEL

Grand Union Canal Company boats **Fornax** *and* **Ra** *at Stoke Bruerne in the 1930s. This famous canal village is located at the head of a flight of seven locks and close to the southern portal of the 3057yd Blisworth Tunnel. Although the Grand Junction Canal, as it was then known, was opened in 1800 the tunnel was not completed until five years later. In the intervening years a tramway linked the two ends of the canal. Within the village itself are attractive thatched cottages, a double arched bridge, the popular canalside Boat Inn and the Waterways Museum. The Museum is housed in a former stone warehouse and the exhibits, including a traditional canal narrow boat, illustrate the 200-year history of English canals.*

*A busy scene in Blisworth cutting on the Grand Junction Canal,
circa 1915. A queue of narrow boats with their crews and towing
horses wait to pass through the long and narrow Blisworth Tunnel
on their journey south to London.*

Workmen carrying out repairs to a tunnel air vent above Blisworth Tunnel in 1910. The air vents were also used to lower materials from the surface to workings in the tunnel. Blisworth is currently the longest navigable canal tunnel in Britain and is located on the Grand Union Canal between the famous canal village of Stoke Bruerne and Blisworth. The 3065yd tunnel is the major engineering feature on the Grand Union and its construction, involving the sinking of 19 shafts, took eight years to complete. During this period an early attempt to bore through the hill was abandoned due to flooding and the present tunnel was not opened until 1805, five years after the rest of the canal was completed. During this period a horse-drawn tramway over the hill linked the two ends of the canal, involving a lengthy delay for commercial traffic. The tunnel was temporarily closed between 1980 and 1984 for a £4 million restoration.

Above: *Internal view of Blisworth Tunnel on the Grand Junction Canal, circa 1910.*

Left: *The northern portal of Blisworth Tunnel, Grand Junction Canal circa 1920, with horse-boat* Lyde. *The tunnel's dimensions only allowed narrowboats to pass through but no towpath was constructed so towing horses had to be led over Blisworth Hill, by way of the path on the left of this photograph, to rejoin the boat at the southern portal. In the early days boats had to be 'legged' through the tunnel until steam tugs were introduced in 1876. The tugs were withdrawn in 1936 when most of the canal craft were diesel-powered.*

BRAUNSTON

Above: *A wonderfully evocative photograph of a canal family and their boats at Braunston Top Lock on the Grand Junction Canal in 1912. This flight of six locks takes the canal down to Braunston, one mile to the west. In 1932 the newly formed Grand Union Canal, with financial assistance from the Government, undertook a massive scheme of widening the 52 locks between Braunston and Birmingham. The western portal of Braunston Tunnel lies ¼-mile to the east.*

Left: *A canal stoppage at Braunston, junction of the Oxford Canal and the Grand Junction Canal, Whitsunday 1922. In the foreground is Samuel Barlow's boat No.12. Barlow's were a major carrier of coal and their boats continued in commercial use until 1970. Their boats were noted for the elaborate hand painted decorations which were painstakingly carried out at the company's Braunston boat yard. Today, Braunston is still a bustling canalside village with a large marina, extensive facilities for modern-day canal boat users and restored canalside buildings. 1¾-miles to the east is the crooked 2042yd Braunston Tunnel, finally completed in 1796 after quicksands were encountered during its construction.*

*A busy scene at Braunston stop lock during widening in
1933. In 1932 the newly-formed Grand Union Canal
embarked on widening the 52 locks between Braunston
and Birmingham. This was part of a major modernisation
scheme to enable wide beam boats to travel from London
to Birmingham. However, when the Government grant
ran out the task was only completed as far as, but not
including, Camp Hill Locks. Thus, the great dream of
wide beam boats being able to travel into the heart of
Britain's second largest city was never realised.*

OXFORD CANAL

A cargo of coal is unloaded from one of Joseph Skinner's boats at the Oxford Canal Basin, circa 1930. Joe Skinner never made the change from horse-drawn boats to motor boats and this owner boatman often preferred mule power to horses. His business as general carrier included carrying parts for Morris cars to the factory at Oxford. The Oxford Canal, designed to connect the industrial Midlands with London via the River Thames, was engineered by James Brindley, Samuel Simcock and Robert Whitworth, and completed in 1790. It's contour-hugging, meandering route, following in part the course of the River Cherwell, was soon outdated and with the opening of the Grand Junction Canal in 1805 its viability was threatened. Because the section between Braunston and Napton was also used jointly by the Grand Junction, the Oxford company charged excessive rates for boats to use this stretch. But by 1830, after suffering several years of declining trade, the Oxford embarked on a massive modernisation programme for the section between Braunston Junction and Hawkesbury Junction, reducing the mileage by 13 miles. This succeeded in extending the canal's profitability into the present century but, as was common with other canal companies, trade eventually declined with competition from railways and roads.

HATTON LOCKS

Above: *A pair of horse-drawn boat sterns at Hatton Locks on the Grand Union Canal in the 1930s. Nellie Freeth is the girl steerer on Samuel Barlow Coal Company's boat* Dragonfly. *The massive flight of 21 locks at Hatton, with their distinctive paddle gear and a rise of 146ft, is one of the wonders of the canal world. As part of the modernisation of the canal, the locks were widened to accommodate wide-beam boats in 1934. It was in October of that year that the Duke of Kent, aboard the boat* Progress, *attended the opening ceremony to mark the completion of the widening scheme.*

Right: *The Freeth boat family pose for the camera halfway up the massive Hatton flight of locks on the Grand Union Canal, circa 1930. The two Samuel Barlow boats are* Caronia *and* Dragonfly.

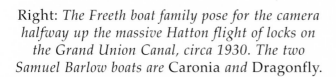

The Duke of Kent arrives aboard the prototype wide boat Progress *at the opening of the wide locks redevelopment, Hatton Top Lock, 1933. The G.U.C.C.Co. planned to operate 60-ton capacity wide beam boats between London and Birmingham but failure to complete the widening scheme throughout meant that the boats never went into production. The diesel-powered* Progress, *built at Tring, spent a few years operating as a maintenance boat and, after several years languishing on the canal bottom, was then converted to a house boat.*

CANALS OF BIRMINGHAM

A busy scene in the 1930s showing Grand Union Canal Company boats Pleione, Fornax, Baldock, Banbury, Stanton *and* Kew *at Sampson Road Wharf in Birmingham. The wharf is located half a mile south east of Bordesley Junction where the Grand Union links up with the Birmingham & Warwick Junction Canal. The six Camp Hill Locks, located immediately to the north west of Sampson Road Wharf, dropping the canal into Birmingham, are narrow and only allow boats of 7ft beam or less to pass through. Although a major lock widening scheme for the whole of the Grand Union was commenced in 1932, funds ran out before Camp Hill Locks were reached and so broad beam boats were never able to travel into the heart of Birmingham.*

Above: *Birmingham & Midland Canal Carrying Company's boats* Barbara *and* Linda *at Gas Street Basin, Birmingham in 1964. This was in the twilight years of commercial canal boat operations on the Birmingham Canal Network. Gas Street Basin, in the heart of the city, once completely overlooked by dark towering warehouses, is now a modern marina surrounded by shiny new buildings. The basin is the junction between the BCN and the Worcester & Birmingham Canal. The latter canal is one of most heavily locked narrow canals in England and although construction commenced in 1791 it was not completed until 1815. Until that date, goods had to be trans-shipped across the famous Worcester Bar in Birmingham, a 7ft physical obstruction between the Birmingham Canal and the Worcester & Birmingham close to Gas Street Basin.*

Right: *A view of the island toll house at Smethwick on the Birmingham Canal Main Line showing narrows for gauging boats, circa 1910. A number of these unique octagonal toll booths were located at major junctions on the Birmingham Canal Navigations until the 1960s. One example is now preserved at the Black Country Museum in Tipton. Canal boats were gauged for tolls by measuring the height of the gunwale above the water line. This measurement corresponded to a list of charges depending upon the type of cargo being carried.*

King's Norton guillotine gate stop lock on the Stratford-upon-Avon Canal, circa 1900. Although this location is now surrounded by the suburban sprawl of Birmingham, the scene today is still very similar. King's Norton is the junction with the Worcester & Birmingham Canal and the stop lock was installed to prevent the water supply flowing from one company's canal to the other. This unusual stop lock, now disused, has two wooden guillotine gates that operated vertically within a steel frame. The Stratford-upon-Avon Canal was built in two sections. The northern section, from King's Norton to Lapworth, opened in 1802, and the southern, from Lapworth to Stratford, opened in 1818. Commercial traffic was initially heavy but competition was soon encountered with the opening of the railways in the 1830s. By 1856 the canal had been bought by the Great Western Railway and by the end of the 19th century commercial traffic had declined substantially. By the end of World War II the southern section was impassable and the northern section saw very little traffic. Closure was imminent in the 1950s but with massive support from the public and the Inland Waterways Association this decision was rescinded and in 1960 the National Trust took over the southern section, completely restoring it by 1964. It thus became the first canal in Britain to be restored by voluntary labour. The attractively rural canal now sees much activity from pleasure cruising.

Unloading side-tipping coal wagons directly into narrow boats, or joeys, at Hednesford, Cannock Extension Canal, circa 1920. This canal was a branch of the Wyrley & Essington Canal and ran for six miles between Pelsall Junction and Cannock. The extension to Cannock was opened in 1858 to serve the local coal mines and coal was transported until the early 1960s. The northern section was eventually closed in 1963 due to subsidence.

FELLOWS, MORTON & CLAYTON

Close up of Fellows, Morton & Clayton butty Urmston *and boatwomen
at Buckby, Grand Junction Canal, 1922. FMC were one of the largest
canal carriers in Britain, being the result of a merger of three separate
Birmingham carriers in 1889. The company was the largest operator of
steam narrow boats from the 1870s until 1920. FMC's boatmen were
nicknamed 'Joshers' after the name of one of the company's founders,
Joshua Fellows. In 1923 the FMC boatmen were involved in a bitter
17-week strike after the company reduced pay and bonuses. This ended
when police were called to Braunston where the company's boats had
been chained together to stop them being used. When canals were
nationalised in 1948 the large fleet of FMC boats were taken over by the
newly-formed British Waterways Board. A well-preserved example of a
FMC steam narrow boat can be seen at the Black Country Museum
in Tipton.*

GLOUCESTER AND SHARPNESS CANAL

Corn porters with their sack trucks at Gloucester Docks, Gloucester & Sharpness Canal, circa 1900. Built to bypass the notoriously dangerous section of the lower reaches of the River Severn, work on the 15¾-mile canal commenced at Gloucester in 1794 but financial shortages led to only 5½ miles being initially built. In 1817 Thomas Telford was asked by the government to make a feasability study for the completion of the route. On his recommendations the government provided sufficient funds and the canal was completed in 1827. When opened, it was for a while the widest and deepest ship canal in the world. The restored warehouses and docks at Gloucester are now home to the National Waterways Museum. The Museum opened in 1988 and is housed on three floors of a handsome Victorian warehouse within which is told the 200 year story of inland waterways via working models, archive film, interactives and hands-on exhibits. Outside, around two sides of the quay, are boats of all shapes and sizes and old railway wagons and wagon turntables.

Tug Stanegarth *manoevring a train of barges at Sharpness Docks in the 1960s. As a destination for sea-going vessels, Sharpness became much more important when the Gloucester & Sharpness Canal was finally opened on 26 April 1827, 34 years after the passing of the Act of Parliament. However, serious problems were encountered during the construction of the dock basin. In 1825, a dam built at Sharpness to protect the dock from the River Severn was demolished by a 33ft-high tide. Although commercial traffic to Gloucester has now virtually disappeared, the docks are still visited by vessels of up to 5,000 tons.*

A sailing ship unloads its cargo of timber at the junction of the old and new Sharpness Docks, circa 1940. In the background the sea wall separates the tidal River Severn and the Gloucester & Sharpness Canal. Spanning both the canal and the river is the 22-span Severn Railway Bridge, opened in 1879, which was, until the opening of the Severn Tunnel in 1886, the shortest railway route between Bristol and South Wales. Unfortunately, this graceful cast-iron structure was badly damaged in November 1959, when an oil tanker collided in thick fog with the bridge and brought down the two spans and killed five men. The bridge was eventually demolished and only the remains of a few stone piers can still be seen at low tide.

SHROPSHIRE UNION CANAL

Above: *Ice boat* **Audlem** *and crew members at Audlem Wharf, Shropshire Union Canal, circa 1900. Ice was a particular problem on canals and only a few inches could halt traffic. Usually constructed of timber hulls plated with iron, ice boats were hauled through the frozen canal by a team of horses. A team of men were carried on the boat to rock it violently from side to side. The forward motion provided by the horses combined with the sideways motion provided by the men cleared a channel through the ice for the wooden hulled canal boats. In later years these primitive boats were replaced by steam and diesel-powered vessels.*

Left: *A tranquil scene of Market Drayton Wharf and the Staffordshire Farmers warehouse, framed by bridge 62, Shropshire Union Canal, circa 1960. The popular Talbot canalside pub is located adjacent to this bridge. The Shropshire Union Railways & Canal Company was formed in 1846 from the amalgamaton of two other existing canals: the Ellesmere & Chester Canal and the Birmingham & Liverpool Junction Canal. During the period from the mid 19th century to the outbreak of World War I the canal system flourished. Decline set in after the war and the whole system was taken over completely by the London & North Western Railway in 1922. Commercial traffic fell even more over the intervening years to World War II as maintenance of the system was reduced and in 1944 most of the branches were abandoned. On the remaining Main Line and Middlewich Branch commercial traffic continued until the 1960s and since then the canal has been a popular cruising waterway.*

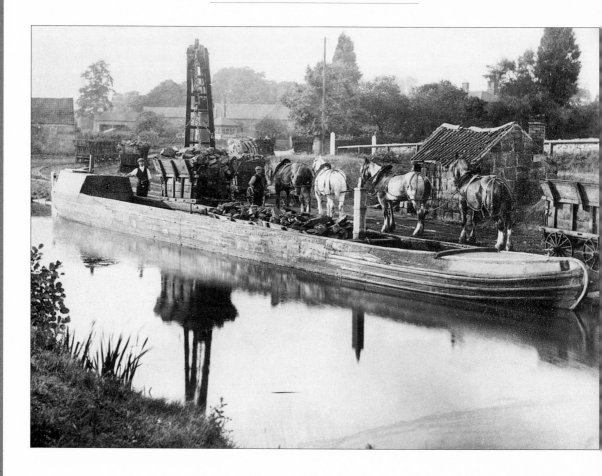

DERBY CANAL

*A narrowboat on the Derby Canal being loaded from
trucks on the Denby to Little Eaton horse-drawn
tramway, circa 1900. The Derby Canal was engineered
by Benjamin Outram and opened in 1796. It linked the
Erewash Canal at Sandiacre, via Derby, with the Trent
& Mersey Canal at Swarkestone, a total of 14½ miles.
A branch to Little Eaton, just over 3 miles in length,
linked with the tramway which served mines and works
in and around Denby. Coal was transported in boxes,
forerunners of modern containers, which were trans-
shipped by crane to the barges at Little Eaton. Due to
the advent of new railway lines traffic soon began to
decline, coal traffic ceasing in 1908 and by 1927 other
commercial traffic had virtually ceased. The whole canal
had been abandoned by 1964.*

CROMFORD CANAL

Cromford Canal Basin showing Wheatcroft & Sons Wharf and the company's boats Onward *and* Bristol, *August 1906. The 14½-mile Cromford Canal was surveyed by William Jessop as a feeder canal linking the quarries and collieries of the Derwent Valley with the Erewash Canal. It was opened in 1794 with 20 locks and a short branch to Pinxton. From 1831 it was linked at Cromford with the Cromford & High Peak Railway which opened up a direct route to Manchester. As with many other canals of the period the Cromford was sold to the local railway, the Midland, in 1852 and from then on the waterway was in decline. Butterley Tunnel, over 3000yds in length, collapsed in 1900, thus effectively closing the canal. Although some local traffic continued, the whole canal became derelict by the 1930s. However, the five mile section from Ambergate to Cromford has now been fully restored, providing a delightful towpath walk. A feature of Cromford Wharf today is the restored Cromford & High Peak Railway Workshops, now in use as a museum.*

TRENT AND MERSEY CANAL

Legging an 'Admiralty' class boat through Barnton Tunnel on the Trent & Mersey Canal in 1960. The boat, owned by Yarwoods, is captained by Jack Jones. Until the introduction of steam tugs, self-propelled boats or towpaths, canal boats were worked through tunnels either by shafting against the roof or sides or more normally by 'legging'. This entailed fixing a pair of special projecting boards on each side of the fore-end of the boat so that the crew, lying on their backs and gripping these boards with their hands, could slowly push their boat through the tunnel by moving their feet against the wall. The 572yd crooked Barnton Tunnel at the northern end of the Trent & Mersey Canal, James Brindley's most ambitious engineering work, was completed in 1777. The canal was a great commercial success and traffic remained heavy until the early 1950s. Regular freight traffic had virtually ceased by the late 1960s.

*An idyllic scene on the Trent & Mersey Canal near Colwich with maintenance motor boat
Oak in October 1957. By this time, commercial traffic on the canal had declined
dramatically. To give some idea of this decline, over one million tons of goods were carried at
the turn of the century but this had shrunk to 24,000 tons by 1959. By the 1960s,
commercial traffic had virtually disappeared but, as part of the Cheshire Ring of canals, the
T&M is now a popular waterway for pleasure cruising.*

HARECASTLE TUNNEL

Above: The air-gauge marker at the entrance to the Harecastle Tunnel, Trent & Mersey Canal, circa 1950. The marker showed the limit for the height of a boat's superstructure.

Left: Boats entering the Kidsgrove end of Harecastle Tunnel, Trent & Mersey Canal, circa 1930. A major feature of the canal at this location is that the water is permanently stained red by the presence of iron in the soil. The Trent & Mersey Canal, partly financed by Josiah Wedgwood and engineered by James Brindley, was completed in 1777. The major engineering feature on the canal was the 2897yd Harecastle Tunnel which took 11 years to build. As there was no towpath provided in the tunnel boats had to be 'legged' through by men lying on their backs. The canal, serving the vast industrial area of the Potteries, was soon stretched to capacity and the tunnel became a major bottleneck. Thomas Telford was contracted to build a second parallel tunnel and this was opened in 1827, each tunnel then being one-way only. This situation ended when the original tunnel had to be closed in the 20th century due to mining subsidence. Electric tugs were introduced in 1914 to speed up freight movement through the tunnel and these continued to operate until the early 1950s.

CANAL BREACHES

Puddling in the bed of the Leeds & Liverpool Canal at Keighley after a breach in 1952. The L&L was completed in 1816 at a cost of £1.2 million and with a length of 127 miles was the longest canal then built in Britain. Due to the construction of wide locks the canal was not adversely affected by the coming of the railways and commercial traffic continued until the early 1960s. Along this stretch of the canal, set in the attractive valley of the River Aire, there are numerous hand-operated swing bridges that considerably slow-down the progress of today's pleasure craft. Close to nearby Granby swing bridge is the National Trust-owned East Riddlesden Hall, an attractive stone manor house and tithe barn built in the 17th-century.

High and dry! A breach near Bryn Howell on the Llangollen Canal in 1960. This scenic and narrow section between Chirk and Llangollen, where the canal hugs the side of the Dee Valley, has seen several major breaches in recent years. The Llangollen Canal runs from Hurleston Junction on the Shropshire Union Canal to Llantisilio in the valley of the River Dee. It was opened throughout in 1806 and its 46-miles contains 21 locks and two major aqueducts, at Chirk and Pontcysyllte. The latter is probably the most impressive canal structure in Britain. The 1000ft-long span was built by Thomas Telford and carries the canal 120ft above the River Dee. Because of its beautiful scenery the Llangollen Canal is now one of the most popular cruising waterways in the country.

A canal burst and subsidence at Marbury on the Trent & Mersey Canal, 21 July 1907. This area was prone to subsidence caused by old rock salt mines which were eroded by water leaking into them. After a period of heavy rain a length of the canal bank collapsed, stranding and badly damaging two narrow boats. One of the boats was carrying a consignment of cheeses, most of which had mysteriously disappeared before the owners could retrieve them. Was this a case of 'Cheese Galore'?

BRIDGEWATER CANAL

Fellows, Morton & Clayton butty Northwich *and a Price & Sons of Birmingham boat at Preston Brook, Bridgewater Canal, circa 1920. Half a mile to the south is the northern end of the crooked Preston Brook Tunnel, 1,239yds in length, and the boundary between the wide-locked Bridgewater Canal and the narrow-locked Trent & Mersey Canal. The Bridgewater Canal, 23½-miles from Preston Brook to Castlefield Junction in Manchester, opened in 1761, and was the first 'modern canal' to be built in Britain. A branch from Preston Brook to Runcorn, where it once linked to the River Mersey via a massive flight of 10 locks, was completed in 1776. Preston Brook was an important trans-shipment point where commercial goods had to be transferred from the Trent & Mersey narrow boats to the wide beam boats of the Bridgewater Canal.*

ANDERTON LIFT

Above: British Waterways' narrow boats, including butty boat Turtle, *waiting at the top of the Anderton Lift on the Trent & Mersey Canal, circa 1960. The Trent & Mersey Canal, partly financed by Josiah Wedgwood and engineered by James Brindley, was completed in 1777. It was designed to provide a link between Liverpool, Manchester and the east coast, via other canals and rivers. Commercially, the Trent & Mersey was a great success, becoming known as the Grand Trunk Canal, and was taken over by the North Staffordshire Railway in 1845. In 1875 the gigantic Anderton Lift was built by Leader Williams, to connect the Trent & Mersey with the River Weaver. Two massive water-filled tanks, originally operated by hydraulic rams, raised or lowered canal boats a distance of 50ft between canal and river. Recently restored, it remains one of the great wonders of the canal world.*

Right: *The massive Anderton Boat Lift soon after the change over to electric power. Originally the hydraulic rams that raised and lowered the water-filled tanks were operated by steam power. In 1908 the lift was modernised and steam power was replaced by electricity.*

MANCHESTER SHIP CANAL

Construction in progress at Eastham Locks on the Manchester Ship Canal in the 1890s. The 36-mile canal, from Eastham on the River Mersey to Manchester was a major engineering triumph when opened by Queen Victoria in 1894. Its dimensions were designed so that sea-going commercial boats, weighing up to 15,000 tons, could travel inland from the River Mersey to a large docks complex in Manchester. Construction took four years and involved the latest excavating machinery available at the time, removing nearly 50 million cubic yards of soil in the process. Apart from the sheer size of excavations, other major engineering features included five sets of giant locks, 600ft long and 80ft wide, and the Bridgewater Canal swing aqueduct and swing road viaduct at Barton. The building of the canal greatly enhanced Manchester's position as one of the leading British industrial cities and until the 1960s large amounts of commercial traffic used the canal. This traffic has declined in recent years and the once mighty docks of Manchester are being redeveloped.

Excavation of a cutting on the Manchester Ship Canal in the 1890s. By the time this canal was being built, mechanisation had truly arrived in the form of steam-powered excavators. 100 of these machines were used in the excavation of the canal, assisted by 173 steam locomotives and 6300 wagons running on 223 miles of temporary railway lines. Over 16,000 navvies were employed, 50 million cubic yards of soil and sandstone rock were excavated and 70 million bricks used in its construction.

ROCHDALE CANAL

Major reconstruction of Piccadilly Lock No. 85 on the Rochdale Canal, Manchester, circa 1880. Of particular interest is the temporary overhead tramway and the traditional navvy costume. The Rochdale Canal, one of three major trans-Pennine canals, was surveyed by John Rennie and engineered by William Jessop. It opened in 1804 and formed an important 33-mile link between the Bridgewater Canal in Manchester and the Calder & Hebble at Sowerby Bridge. Its 92 wide locks were constructed to allow passage of a wide beam barge or two narrow boats side-by-side. Until the mid 19th century the canal was commercially successful but decline set in due to competition from the railways. The last commercial boat passed along its length in 1937 and, although not nationalised in 1948, it was officially abandoned in 1952. With the revival of the Ashton and Peak Forest Canals during the 1970s the short section within Manchester was restored to provide a link in the Cheshire Ring, now much used by pleasure craft. The rest of the canal, which passes through dramatic Pennine scenery and which provides for a spectacular towpath walk, is now the subject of full scale restoration.

LANCASTER CANAL.

THE SWIFT
PACKET BOATS
SAIL DAILY,

TWICE in each direction between PRESTON and KENDAL, and THREE TIMES
in each direction between LANCASTER and PRESTON,

IN CONNEXION WITH THE RAILWAY TRAINS.

SOUTHWARDS.

From	H. M.	H. M.	H. M.	MILES
KENDAL	6 30		8 30	
Crooklands	7 30	9	30	
Holme	7 45	9	45	
Tewitfield	8 30		10 30	
Carnforth	8 55	10	55	
Bolton	9 5	11	5	
Hest Bank	9 30	11	30	
LANCASTER	6 0	9 50	11 50	
Galgate	6 20	10 20	12 20	
Cliffton Hill	6 45	10 45	12 45	
Garstang	7 20	11 20	1 20	
Bilsbrow	7 50	11 50	1 50	
Swillbrook	8 15	12 15	2 15	
Salwick	8 25	12 25	2 25	
Arrive Preston	8 30	1 30	3 30	

NORTHWARDS.

From	H. M.	H. M.	H. M.	MILES
PRESTON	11 0		1 30	5 0
Salwick	11 35	5	5	5
Swillbrook	11 45	7	15	5 45
Bilsbrow	12 10	2	40	6 10
Garstang	12 40	17	3 10	6 40
Cliffton Hill	1 15	12	3 45	7 15
Galgate	1 40	25	4 10	7 40
LANCASTER	2 20	30	4 50	8 20
Hest Bank	3 0	14	5 30	
Bolton	3 15	34	5 45	
Carnforth	3 25	58	5 55	
Tewitfield	3 50	45	6 20	
Holme	4 40	44	7 10	
Crooklands	4 55	43	7 25	
Arrive at Kendal	6 20	57	8 50	

FARES.

	First Cabin.	Second Cabin.
Between KENDAL and LANCASTER, or LANCASTER and PRESTON	3s.	2s.

THE RAILWAY TRAINS

From PRESTON	9 45 morning		From LIVERPOOL	8 45 morning
Do.	2 20 afternoon		Do.	11 0 do.
			Do.	2 30 afternoon
Do.	4 20 afternoon		MANCHESTER	9 0 morning
			Do.	11 15 do.
			Do.	2 45 afternoon

FORM DIRECT CONVEYANCES WITH THE PACKET BOATS.

The Railway Trains at 9 45 and 2 20 are in immediate connexion with the GRAND JUNCTION TRAINS from Manchester.

Omnibuses between the Packets and the Railway.

Coaches to and from Bolton and Chorley, meet the Packets at the Canal Wharf, Preston.

Parcels carefully conveyed and delivered free of Porterage.—It is particularly requested that all Parcels for any place between Preston and Kendal, sent by the Railway Trains, should be marked "To be forwarded by Canal Packets."—Small Parcels between Preston and Lancaster, or Lancaster and Kendal, charged only SIXPENCE each, other distances equally moderate.

CANAL OFFICE, LANCASTER, JUNE, 1839.

ORRELL, PRINTER, PRESTON.

LANCASTER CANAL PACKET BOATS

Timetable of the Lanaster Canal packet boat, Waterwitch II, in 1839. After cessation of the packet boat service she became an inspection boat and continued in service as such until 1930. Before the advent of the railways, fast passenger boat services were introduced in 1804, between Preston and Kendal, covering the journey in a leisurely 7 hours. The 41-mile long canal was originally envisaged as a route from Kendal to Wigan. A northern section from Tewitfield to Preston and an unconnected section from Clayton to Chorley were completed by 1799. The missing five miles was never built. Instead, a horse-drawn tramway, crossing the River Ribble on a large wooden bridge, linked the two unconnected sections of the canal. The major engineering work of the northern section is the impressive Lune Aqueduct which carries the canal over the river at Lancaster on five 60ft-high stone arches. The southern section was extended to join with the Leeds & Liverpool Canal and the rest of the northern section to Kendal was completed by 1819. The canal is connected to the sea by a short branch, opened in 1826, from the main line south of Lancaster to Glasson Docks. This is still the canal's only access to the outside world. Meanwhile the tramway linking the two sections was closed in 1857, thus permanently sealing the fate of the original scheme. Following the pattern set by many other canals the northern route was sold to the London & North Western Railway in 1885. The section from Tewitfield Locks to Kendal was abandoned in 1955 and subsequently permanently blocked by the M6 motorway.

STANDEDGE TUNNEL

The Marsden end of Standedge Tunnel on the Huddersfield Narrow Canal in the 1950s. Immediately behind and above the canal tunnel entrance are the portals of the later railway tunnel. Completed in 1811 as a trans-Pennine link, the Huddersfield Narrow Canal involved major engineering work over its 20-mile length to a junction with the Ashton Canal in Manchester. This involved the construction of 74 locks, 10 reservoirs and the 5698yd Standedge Tunnel. The tunnel, the longest in Britain, has three passing places, 600ft-deep ventilation shafts and a summit 650ft above sea level. As there was no towing path boats had to be 'legged' through, a process which took three and a half hours. Expensive and slow to operate, the canal was soon in competition with the newly constructed railways into whose ownership it passed in 1844. Most traffic had ceased by the early part of this century and the last complete passage was made in 1940. The canal was officially abandoned in 1944 but is now the scene of a major restoration project. The Huddersfield Canal Society was formed in 1974 and since then over two-thirds of the canal has been restored.

LEEDS AND LIVERPOOL CANAL

One of the wonders of British canals viewed from the top: the Bingley Five Rise locks under repair, circa 1915. These wide-beam staircase locks on the Leeds & Liverpool Canal were built of millstone grit in 1774 and lift boats a height of 60ft. Great care has to be taken when operating them as it is not possible to drain a lock until the one below is completely empty. Failure to follow this procedure can result in a spectacular tidal wave that gushes forth to the lower part of the canal. Just over two miles along the canal to the east is the famous estate village of Saltaire, built in 1850 by Sir Titus Salt.

A tranquil scene on the Leeds & Liverpool Canal at the turn of the century. Short boat **Tiger** *with crew and horse pose for the camera. The building of this major trans-Pennine route was a long and drawn-out affair and on its completion was the longest single canal in Britain. Construction started in 1770 and incorporated part of the former River Douglas Navigation but the final route was not completed until 1816. On the western side, the Leeds & Liverpool joined with part of the doomed southern section of the Lancaster Canal between Johnson's Hill and Wigan. The Leigh Branch, linking with the Bridgewater Canal, opened in 1820 and the short link with Liverpool Docks was built in 1846. Major engineering features included the 23 flight of locks at Wigan, the 1640yd Foulridge Tunnel and the flight of five staircase locks at Bingley. The canal's continuing success well into the 20th century, despite competition from railways, was due to the early decision to build the canal large enough for wide boats.*

A school trip on the Leeds & Liverpool Canal in 1934. The cost per head was 1/6d (7½p) and for insurance purposes the passengers had to 'sign their life away'! The happy, smiling faces set off for their exciting voyage on the boat Skelter.

Suction unloading the motorised short boat **Romabate** *at Tate & Lyle's factory in Liverpool, the western terminus of the Leeds & Liverpool Canal, circa 1960. The sugar factory was once one of the most important users of water transport in the area. Commercial traffic on the L&L lasted well into the 1960s due to the wide locks that were built during the initial construction of the canal in the early 19th century. Although the main line of the canal was completed by 1816, the short cut down into Liverpool's Stanley Docks was not made until 1846. Access to this industrial section of the canal in Liverpool today is difficult due to the lack of a public towpath.*

TOM PUDDINGS ON THE AIRE & CALDER NAVIGATION

Coal-laden 'Tom Puddings' hauled by a steam tug on the Aire & Calder Navigation in 1930. Up to nineteen of these compartment boats were linked together to form a train that could be mechanically loaded and unloaded. They were introduced to the Aire & Calder in 1864 and modern versions of these compartment boats still carry coal from Yorkshire pits to Ferrybridge Power Station on this commercially active waterway. The modern 'Tom Puddings' are propelled by a diesel tug pushing a train of three, 170-ton capacity compartment boats.

FORTH AND CLYDE CANAL

Passenger pleasure steamer Gipsy Queen *at Craigmarloch, Forth & Clyde Canal, 1939. The 35-mile long Forth & Clyde Canal, from Bowling Harbour on the River Clyde to Grangemouth, was a useful route that linked the east and west coasts of central Scotland and was opened in 1790. A major engineering feature of the canal is the magnificent stone viaduct over the River Kelvin near Glasgow. All overbridges had moveable sections that enabled the passage of tall-masted vessels and commercial traffic was carried until the canal's untimely closure in 1962. Although subsequently blocked in many places the canal is being restored and several sections are now used by pleasure boats.*

Pleasure steamers May Queen *and* Fairy Queen *at their moorings at Craigmarloch, Forth & Clyde Canal, 1939.*

CALEDONIAN CANAL

Steam paddle boat **Glengarry** *at Muirton Locks on the Caledonian Canal, circa 1910. The 60-mile canal, from Clachnaharry on the Beauly Firth, near Inverness, to Corpach, near Fort William is actually a series of natural lochs, including 23-mile long Loch Ness, linked together by man-made cuts. It was designed by William Jessop and constructed jointly by him and Thomas Telford. First opened to boats in 1822 and eventually deepened throughout by 1847, its completion allowed ships to travel across Scotland from east to west, and vice versa, without having to make the dangerous sea voyage around Cape Wrath. Although the large locks were built to take vessels up to 150ft long and 35ft in beam the canal was never a financial success. Today the canal is used mainly by fishing boats and pleasurecraft.*

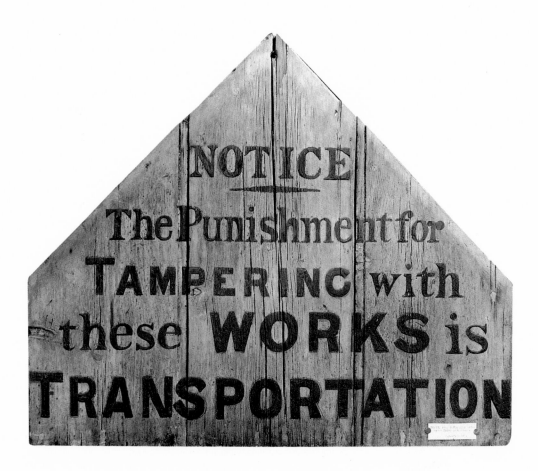

A SIGN OF THE TIMES

This dire warning notice was once attached to South Mill Lock on the Lee & Stort Navigation. Convicts, many of whom had been found guilty of fairly minor crimes by today's standards, were first transported to Australia in 1788. This practice eventually ended in 1868.